Grandmas Never Leave Us®

Story by Billy Light
Illustrations by Lindsey Light (Age 8)

Our children, Lindsey and Andrew, lost both of their Grandmothers to cancer within the same year.

How could this be happening? My wife and I had a very hard time understanding their deaths, so how do we explain their dying to our young children?

We told them this story and our children speak of their Grandmas and even speak to their Grandmas all the time. Even their friends are reminded and now look up to their own Grandma's Star!

I hope this story can help soften the reality and finality of death to a loved one. This book is written for your children… and for you.

Billy Light

This is the story of Lindsey and Andrew, Daddy and Mommy, and their beautiful Grandmother.

Lindsey and Andrew loved their Grandmother very, very much! To Grandma, her two grandchildren were her whole life.

Mommy and Daddy had to tell them not to have **too much fun!**

They spent the night at her house. She took them to parades and to the circus. She baked cakes for their birthday parties.

Spending time with Grandma was like being on vacation.

They could not wait to see her again.

One day, Grandma started feeling weak and tired. She began getting very sick. Lindsey and Andrew drew pictures and made cards to help Grandma feel better.

Daddy visited Grandma every day and brought Lindsey and Andrew over to give Grandma big hugs. Grandma would smile, but the kids knew Grandma was very sick.

They were her best medicine.

They talked to Daddy and Mommy about Grandma dying.

Could it be possible? What is dying? Do Daddy and Mommy even know?

Daddy tried to prepare the children for the sad times that were to follow.

Grandma went to the hospital and stayed for a while, but she never came home…

…GRANDMA DIED

Mommy and Daddy cried. Lindsey and Andrew cried.

They had not seen their parents crying before. They were very sad.

Soon though, Daddy began to smile. He realized where Grandma was and why GOD had brought Grandma to live with him in heaven.

Grandma was so sick for so long and she could not get better. GOD did not want Grandma to hurt anymore.
He wanted her to be free of pain and happy.

No more suffering!!

Daddy and the kids had long discussions about where Grandma was living now. Her body was so sick that GOD took her away from it. She was the biggest, brightest star in the sky.

You can look up to her and talk to her anytime. She is always around with us. She can't talk to us, but she is always listening. She is always smiling on us and laughing with us.

She will never leave us. She loves us so much.

She is probably even the boss of heaven!!!

Andrew and Lindsey's friends even talk about their Grandma's star in the sky. They have shown everybody her star. They are very proud of her star.

They will always follow it and look up to her!

So, on a clear night, no matter where you are, look up to the sky at the stars. You will see the biggest, brightest, and shiniest star in the sky…

…and Lindsey and Andrew will tell you whose star it is.

It's their Grandma's star.

She is always there and she will never, **ever** leave us!!!

If we love the ones who leave us,
then the ones we love never leave us.

Hello,

My name is Lindsey Light. My dad and I wrote this book over 20 years ago when I was almost 8 years old. I remember my grandmothers being very sick at the same time and in different hospitals. My brother, Andrew, and I would draw pictures and get-well cards for them to hang in their rooms because our dad told us how happy it made them and we wanted them to know they were always on our minds. Sometimes we would sing on a cassette tape that my parents could play for them on their daily visits. It was such a sad time, but I remember thinking we were helping them feel better, and they were the most popular grandmas in the whole hospital!

Now I am 29 years old and I grew up without my Grandmas. My brother and I always talk about how we missed out on having grandmas like our friends did. I still remember when my dad had me draw pictures for his story because at the time I wanted to grow up to be an artist. It was fun to draw the pictures and remember all the good times, but it was also a learning experience!! During the process we asked all kinds of questions about my grandmothers and what was happening to them. My dad tried his best to explain why they were sick, as only a parent can, to his still-developing children. Then they died.

This story had been hiding in a drawer for over 20 years!! This past year, my husband, Michael and I put the story into book form for my dad's birthday. To see the happy tears running down my dad's face when he read it was so amazing. We were able to bring the story back to life - if only we could do the same for my grandmas!

It is our hope that by sharing our story with adults and children alike, we can help you get through what we know is a tough time. Experiencing loss is never easy, but it definitely helped us and we will always have a beautiful reminder of our beloved grandmas.

It really is true, Grandmas Never Leave Us!

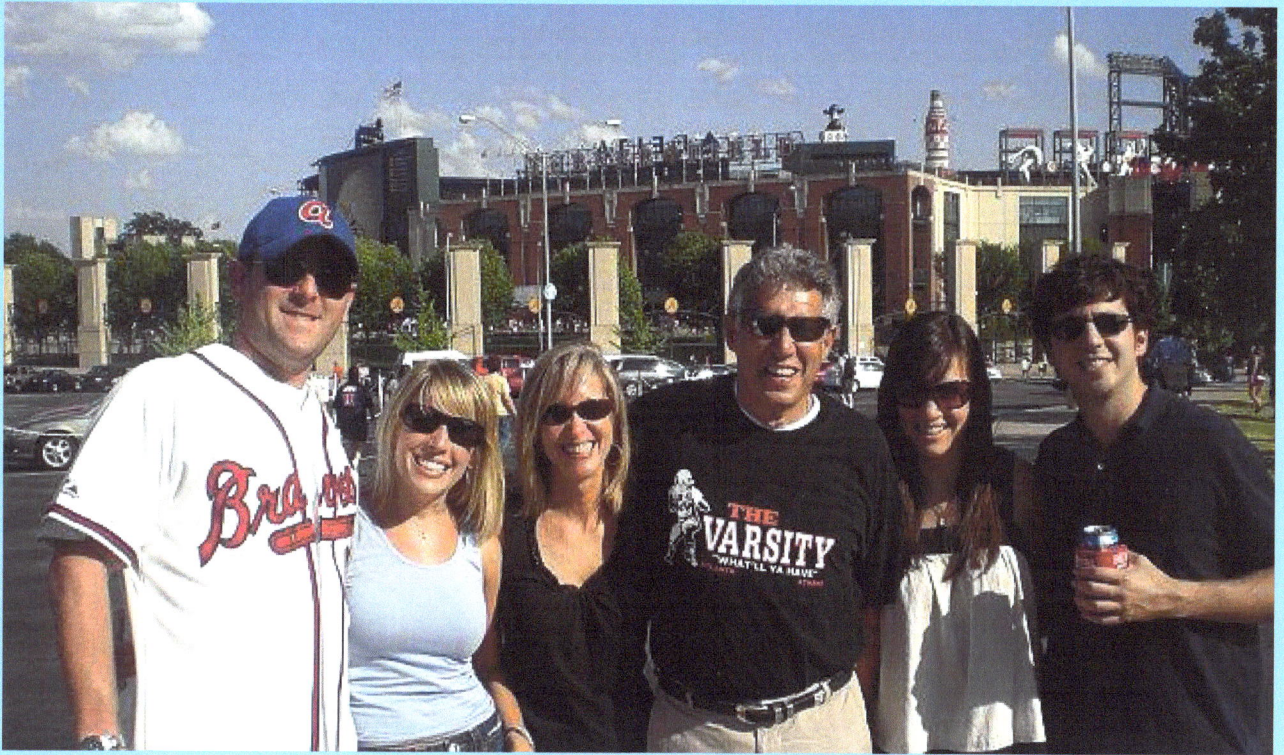

Michael   Lindsey   Lynn   Billy   Molly   Andrew

Dedicated in memory of:
"Grandma Louise" and "Grandma Shirley."

Thank you for sharing in our story.

This book is even more about *your* story.

Whether you're giving this book to help a friend or for yourself, we hope you'll write your own thoughts about your special loved one in these next few pages...

Add Your Loved One to Our Story:

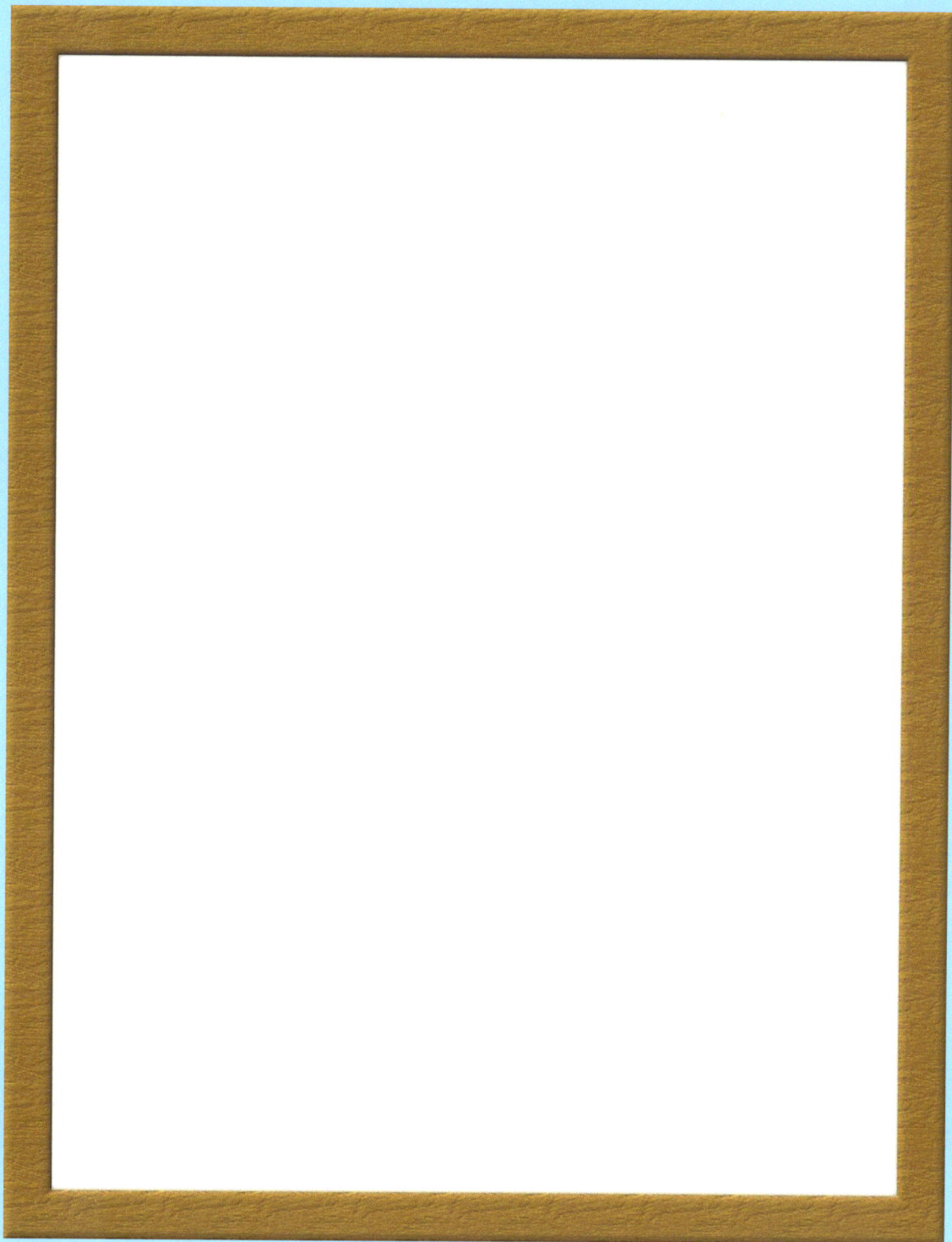

MEMORIES

www.ingramcontent.com/pod-product-compliance
Lightning Source LLC
Chambersburg PA
CBHW042110040426

42448CB00002B/215